SHAWN MENDES
Superstar Next Door

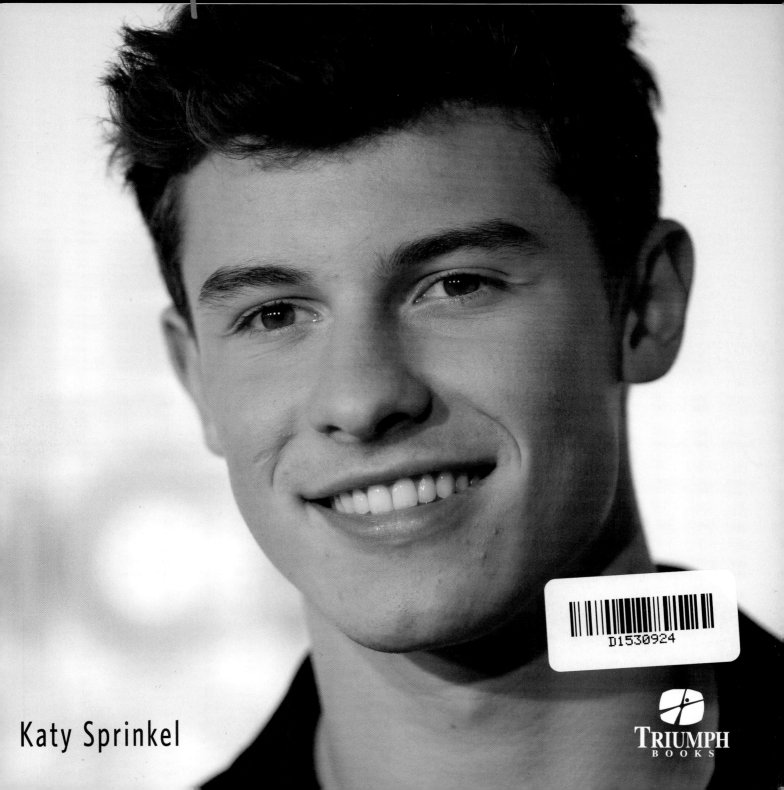

Katy Sprinkel

TRIUMPH BOOKS

This book is available in quantity at special discounts for your group or organization. For further information, contact:

Triumph Books LLC
814 North Franklin Street
Chicago, Illinois 60610
(312) 337-0747
www.triumphbooks.com

Printed in U.S.A.
ISBN: 978-1-62937-376-8
Written, developed, and packaged by Katy Sprinkel

Design and page production by Patricia Frey
Cover design by Andy Hansen

Chapter-opening photo courtesy of iStock.com; all remaining photos courtesy of AP Images.

CONTENTS

Life of the Party

Shawn does a stripped-down performance for fans in London.

He's talented. He's tech-savvy. He's a teenager. And he's taking the world by storm. Shawn already has a #1 album, his full-length debut *Handwritten*, has had six singles (and counting) crack the Billboard 100, and headlined a world tour. Not bad for a kid who just graduated high school.

He's been hailed by critics and fans alike as the next Justin Bieber, a comparison he accepts with a humbleness beyond his years. "Being compared to him is great," he told Digital Spy. "He is super talented."

And surely, the two Canadians have plenty in common. For starters, they both owe their start to the Internet. Justin was famously discovered after posting YouTube videos of himself singing covers of various pop and R&B songs, and quickly found a record deal with RBMG, headed by Usher—one of the very artists he covered. We all know the rest of the story.

Shawn, a self-taught singer and guitarist, has been called the first Vine superstar. But in an Internet landscape where every YouTube cover artist is aiming to be "discovered," becoming a world-famous musician isn't what Shawn set out to be. Instead, he started posting six-second snippets on Vine just to amuse himself and his friends. It was "a habit and a fun thing to do after school in a boring town," he told *Rolling Stone*.

Indeed, it wasn't until he started to get a response that he started to think bigger. He posted a short cover of a lesser-known Justin Bieber ballad and it got attention immediately—he was literally an overnight success. "I posted this little six-and-a-half-second clip of me singing.... I woke up the next morning and I had like 10,000 followers.... I was like, *Okay, I guess I should go with this*," he told KiSS-FM. Before long, he was one of the most popular contributors on Vine.

He kept on posting, and the social media momentum kept on building. Soon, his followers were requesting songs for him to sing. They were telling their friends,

119,000

BY THE NUMBERS

The number of copies of Handwritten *sold in the first week, reaching #1 on the Billboard 200.*

building fan sites devoted to him, making their own tributes.

Vine isn't a logical path to stardom, Shawn admits, but it worked for him. "People could say, 'Well, it doesn't take much talent to put a six-second video up," he told the *New York Times*. "I would argue that it does, because you only have six seconds to impress somebody," he said. "And if you can do that in six seconds, then you've done a good job."

He started gaining momentum across other social media platforms, too, including Instagram, Facebook, Twitter, and, yes, YouTube, where fans could find more than six seconds of Shawn at a time. It was on YouTube that he got the attention of now-manager Andrew Gertler, who was searching online for artists covering A Great Big World's smash hit "Say Something" and randomly stumbled across Shawn's version. Gertler rushed to sign Shawn, and soon there was a record deal in place with Island Records. "There was something about him that just struck me as different from every other kid on social media," Gertler told AXS.com. "Not only was his voice unique, but he had a natural charisma that I don't think you can learn. Something just draws people to him."

It's that relatability that fans echo when they talk about him, too. He really does feel like the superstar next door. He could

> " You only have six seconds to impress somebody [on Vine]. And if you can do that in six seconds, then you've done a good job. "

Shawn performs for his hometown crowd on WE Day 2015 in Toronto.

*Shawn takes home
Teen Choice honors.*

be their neighbor, their classmate, their best friend. And in many ways, Shawn is still a typical teenage guy. He plays sports and writes poetry and eats junk food and worries about acne. He just also happens to have a surging music career.

He released his first single, "Life of the Party," in 2014 and it hit big, selling almost 150,000 copies in its first week and sailing to #24 on the Billboard charts. It was a huge smash for Shawn, who hadn't had *any* radio play to promote the single. None. Zilch. Nada. All the promotion was done through his social media sites. "We decided to put it online with no marketing or airplay because we wanted to understand his fan base and how it would behave," Island head David Massey told Billboard. "We released the song at 11:15 PM, and it was #1 at midnight. Within the first 24 hours, we had exceeded 100,000. That's true fan engagement and true conversion, from being a fan to putting down money."

WHOLE LOTTA BLING

Just 18 and already Shawn has earned a full trophy case. Something tells us he's going to have a whole lot more before he's through.

Much Music Awards

MTV Europe Awards

Kids' Choice/ Teen Choice Awards

People's Choice Award

Shorty Award

It's a feat most artists wouldn't dare to attempt. What's more, it made Shawn the youngest artist ever to break the Billboard Top 25 with a debut single. It was also the best debut single for any act since *American Idol* winner Phillip Phillips released "Home" in 2012. (Of course, he had his own publicity from the show to help him out!)

"This is all happening so fast," Shawn told Fuse in 2014. "A few months ago I wasn't this popular and people didn't know about my music, and now all of the sudden there are screaming girls down the block. They're singing my songs live. It's unbelievable."

Fans everywhere were smitten for Shawn. No surprise, then, that he was handpicked by none other than Taylor Swift to be the opener on the North American leg of her *1989* world tour. The megastar is famous for being hands-on when it comes to her opening acts, and has played a role in launching the careers of now-huge singers like Ed Sheeran, Austin Mahone, and Florida Georgia Line, among others. So what was it like getting the call that he would be opening to packed stadiums for basically the biggest pop artist in the world? "I'm blown away," he told MTV. It "is the coolest tour I could possibly be on ever. You can't really beat that tour so that was the biggest news," he said.

Playing to packed stadiums from coast to coast, Shawn was thrown into the

fanchat

"Shawn is a good role model, even kids can look up to him bc he's such a good example to everyone."

—@mendestayed via Twitter

Taking selfies with fans in Toronto.

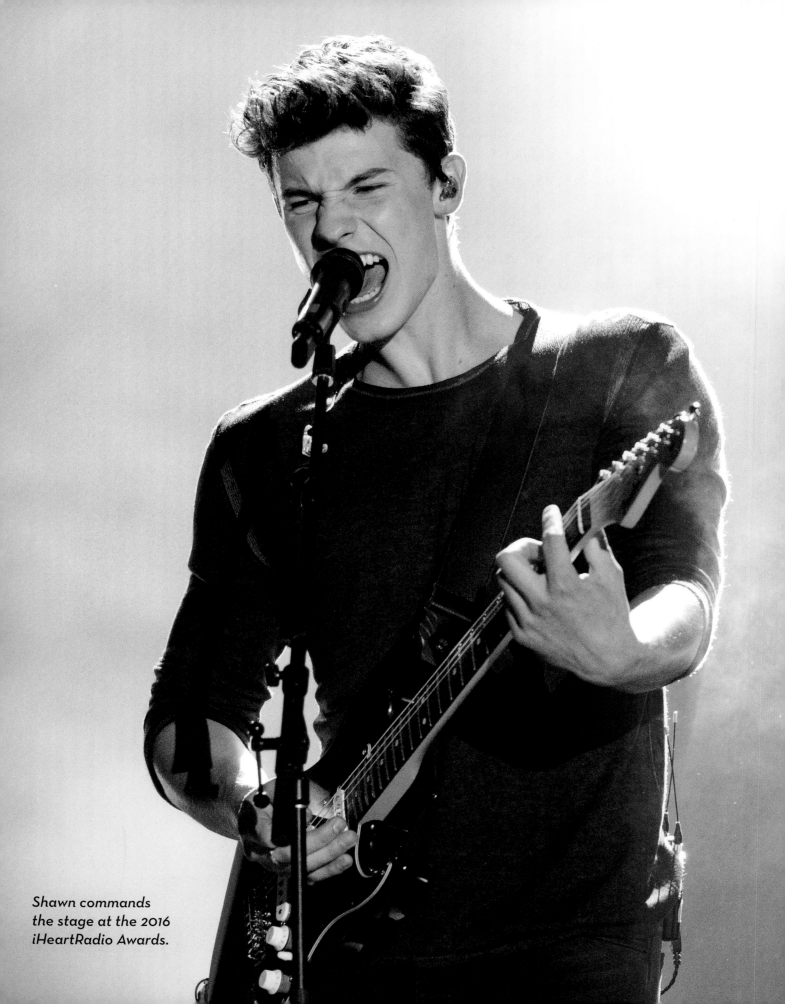

Shawn commands the stage at the 2016 iHeartRadio Awards.

deep end. And he had to learn how to swim—fast. He was a long way from Ontario.

To call it a whirlwind success would be an understatement. "What a year. It's been completely surreal for me," Shawn told Mix 104.1 in Boston. He was already a huge fan of Swift, so to be tapped by her was even more of an honor for the fledgling artist. "[Just a year ago,] I was listening to Taylor Swift's 'Our Song,' knowing every single lyric to that song and not thinking that one day I would be playing in front of a stadium for her," he continued.

His debut album, *Handwritten*, was released in April 2015, just a month before he hit the road with Swift. It shot straight to #1, thanks again to Shawn's grassroots fan base, who rallied to make the album a smash in its first week. Shawn was the youngest artist to reach #1 in nearly five years, since Justin Bieber hit pay dirt with *My World 2.0.* (Mendes was 16 years and 8 months when he hit #1; Justin was 16 and 2 months.)

RECORD BREAKER

15 YEARS, 11 MONTHS, 4 DAYS

That's how old Shawn was when he first hit the charts, debuting "Life of the Party" at #24 on the Billboard 100. The appearance made him the youngest artist ever to debut on the Billboard Top 25.

Life of the Party

Comparisons aside, Shawn isn't living in the Biebs' shadow by any means. He's no pop confection. It's not about the elaborate staging, the dance numbers, the pyrotechnics. With him, it's all about the music. Shawn sees himself as a singer-songwriter, influenced by artists such as John Mayer and Ed Sheeran. His focus is always, first and foremost, on the music. His sophomore album, 2016's *Illuminate*, illustrates just how much he's matured as an artist.

When asked by VH1 about his 10-year plan, he responded with his characteristic humility. "I'm always wary on trying to guess. Hopefully I'm still on stage, but if not I'm sure I'll be writing songs somewhere. I'm never going to stop doing music." Indeed, it's his dedication to his craft that's gotten him this far.

Whatever he's doing, it seems to be working. Ask anyone in the Mendes Army and they'll tell you that the best is yet to come. ★

TOP OF THE POPS

Shawn has already had six singles reach the Billboard 100. But with the release of *Illuminate* he's poised to have even more hits. Here's a breakdown of how he's done so far.

Song	Date	Peaked At
"Stitches"	November 15, 2015	4
"Treat You Better"	September 3, 2016	12
"I Know What You Did Last Summer" (with Camila Cabello)	January 30, 2016	20
"Life of the Party"	July 12, 2014	24
"Something Big"	January 17, 2015	80
"A Little Too Much"	February 21, 2015	94

Shawn performs "Stitches" at the Billboard Music Awards in 2016.

O, Canada

Chapter Two:
O, Canada

The first thing you notice about Pickering, Ontario, is how pretty it is. Situated on the northern shore of Lake Ontario, it boasts beautiful waterfront views from its beaches and park spaces. Just 40 kilometers east of the city of Toronto (that's 25 miles, for you American readers!), Pickering is a quiet bedroom community of about 90,000 citizens at last census. And among them is none other than Shawn!

Shawn Peter Raul Mendes was born on August 8, 1998, in nearby Toronto. His mother, Karen, is from England and his father, Peter, is Portuguese. (Shawn's second middle name is a nod to his Portuguese heritage.) A sister, Aaliyah, came along five years later.

His parents both worked—his mom as a real estate agent and his dad as an entrepreneur in the restaurant supply business—but they were always spending time together as a family. Shawn is still extremely close with his parents and sister, whom he credits as the key to his success. "They're involved with everything I do," he told the *Telegraph*.

fanchat

"I am now 14 and I've been with Shawn since I was 11, through everything!... He has accomplished so much and it makes me sad that he isn't 'our little secret' anymore.... I will ALWAYS support Shawn and I'm excited to see what the future brings him!!! :)"

—Kayla Da Costa via YouTube

Performing at the 2014 US Open Arthur Ashe Kids Day at Flushing Meadows, New York.

Giving back at a benefit for the Salvation Army in 2014.

In fact, it was his sister who had a huge hand in getting his career started in the first place. "My sister recorded like the first 50 Vines I ever did," including the fateful Bieber cover, he told Fusion. "She has to get cred." Later on, the two of them began to record videos of themselves singing together.

There was always lots of love—and fun—to spare in the Mendes home. His parents definitely had a playful side. One holiday ruled over the rest, and it's not what you might think. "My dad takes Halloween serious," Shawn told PopBuzz. "At our house we always dress up and create scenes—like murder scenes. It takes like

DID YOU KNOW?

Way back in November 2013, Shawn was named Pine Ridge Secondary School's "Face of the Future" for being "an accomplished singer and performer." He was already getting the attention of Internet audiences, as well as playing locally in Toronto. How right their prediction was!

TRUE OR FALSE?

Shawn can speak three languages.

FALSE! THOUGH THIS RUMOR HAS BEEN WIDELY REPORTED, SHAWN SET THE RECORD STRAIGHT. HE SPEAKS ONLY ENGLISH, THOUGH HE'D LOVE TO BE FLUENT IN OTHER LANGUAGES SOMEDAY.

three weeks. It was always a fun thing as a kid."

And there was always music playing at home. His parents, an early influence on Shawn's taste, had a wide range of musical likes, from country music to reggae to rock 'n' roll. It was as typical to hear the heavy guitars of Led Zeppelin in the house as it was to hear the twang of Garth Brooks.

But while his folks kept the music on steady rotation, neither of them had ever picked up an instrument themselves. Shawn, on the other hand, gravitated toward music and performing. He was a member of the glee club at Pine Ridge Secondary School, and took acting lessons. (To the surprise of no one, he

CANADA IS CRUSHING IT!

Shawn and Justin are far from the only Canadians burning up the US charts right now. Here are a few other artists you might not know are Canucks.

Drake

Before Drizzle became an R&B superstar, he was an actor on Canada's most famous television export, Degrassi.

The Weeknd

Abel Makkonen Tesfaye, better known as the Weeknd, has had two #1 singles and worked with artists from Kanye West to Ariana Grande.

Carly Rae Jepsen

"Call Me Maybe," eh? This pop star hails from British Columbia.

Michael Buble

The crooner already has four Grammys and three #1 albums under his belt.

played Prince Charming in one production.) He learned to play the piano and goofed around with his friends making music and just chilling out.

As Shawn started to develop his own musical tastes, he began to gravitate toward one artist in particular. "My friends and I think John Mayer is this music god," he told *Seventeen*. "We've grown up learning from [him]." Those who know Shawn's music well can see John Mayer's fingerprints there (but more on Mayer's influence later).

He credits Pickering with giving him inspiration as a songwriter. Among other things, it allowed him to dream big. "Growing up in a suburban home the world seems so massive to you. It seems like cities are so big and so far away and there's so much in them. So your imagination runs wild," he told the *Toronto Globe and Mail*.

It was by all counts a normal and happy early life. He spent his days playing football (or, as they

Taking a break in between songs at a performance in Baltimore.

Shawn gives the audience a Merry Christmas at the 2014 Z100 Jingle Ball.

say in America, soccer) and longboarding with buddies, or just running around the neighborhood. And, like most kids, he'd occasionally get into hot water with his parents. "When I was young, one of my best friends threw a ball through my garage window and I took the blame for him. And I got into huge trouble until a couple of years later when I told my dad it wasn't me," he told MTV.

And, like many Canadian boys, he learned how to play hockey. Only it didn't go so well at first. "The first year I started hockey I didn't know how to skate, so I got

on the ice with all of the hockey players and we were doing drills where we had to go backwards in figure eights. And I could not skate, and I just kept falling on my butt and it was very embarrassing," he confessed to MTV.

He's also a confessed *Harry Potter* nut. "*Harry Potter* is playing 24/7 at my

PICKERING: A HOTBED FOR TALENT

Neil Young

One of the greatest rock musicians of all time, he lived in Pickering for a little while as a child.

Spider Jones

The boxer-turned-humanitarian is a three-time Golden Gloves champion.

Sean Avery

Arguably the town's biggest NHL success story, Avery played 12 seasons with the New York Rangers and three other teams.

Chapter Two:
O, Canada

house," he confessed to fans on Twitter. He's read all of the books and seen the movies countless times. He references it constantly on social media. He might even have a crush on one of the characters in the films (here's looking at you, Hermione). And which house of Hogwarts would he be in? "Gryffindor, duh!" he told BuzzFeed.

He has a big crew of guys he still calls his best friends today. "I've been friends with the same five guys for eight years now, so being able to go through all this with them has been incredible," he told the BBC in 2015. "They've known that [making music] has been a dream of mine forever, so for it all to happen in front of them is amazing and they've been so supportive. The best part is, they treat me the same as they did before. So I'm no different in my friends' group."

Though life on the road has taken him away from school, he's managed to keep up with his studies. He had a tutor on tour and did courses online. He also got to have a little fun with his high school classmates, attending his school's prom. And in May 2016 he graduated with his class. To mark the muggle rite of passage, he updated his Twitter account to read "Hogwarts graduate. Full-time wizard now."

He was recently asked what advice he'd give to his younger self, telling BANG Showbiz, "I'd probably tell myself to shut up sometimes and stop being such an annoying little brat and be thankful to your parents because they do so much for you.... And I would have told myself to start playing guitar a lot younger [he only started playing at 13]."

He's traveled the globe, but no matter where he goes, there's no place like home. "As soon as I get into Canada and I'm on the roads, I feel like I'm at home," he told Just Jared Jr. "You get that home feeling. It's a really comforting feeling. That's what I miss when I'm away." ★

Shawn visits Philadelphia's Q102 radio to promote Handwritten.

SHAWN VS. JUSTIN

Sure, they get compared to one another all the time, but other than being young and hugely successful Canadian singers, what do the two have in common? Turns out, less than you think.

	SHAWN	JUSTIN
Age discovered?	15	12
Social media of choice?	Vine	YouTube
Musical influences?	John Mayer, Ed Sheeran	Usher, Ne-Yo, Michael Jackson, Justin Timberlake
Instruments played?	Guitar, piano	Guitar, piano, drums, trumpet
Writes his own songs?	Almost always	Sometimes
Does he dance?	"Terribly."	Yes, very well
What would he be if he wasn't a singer?	Actor	Astronaut
Biggest fear?	Open water	Claustrophobia
Sport of choice?	Hockey	Basketball
What does he do in his downtime?	Work out	Work out
Lucky charm	A stuffed lion named Leo	Himself!
Celebrity crush?	Rachel McAdams	Beyoncé, Rihanna
Loves to eat?	Chinese food, muffins	Sour Patch Kids
Won't touch?	Tomatoes	Asparagus
Hidden talent?	"Instaroke" (that's instant karaoke, for those not in the know!)	He can solve a Rubik's Cube

Shawn performs for the plaza at Today in June 2016.

CHAPTER THREE

Six Seconds to Stardom

Singing from the heart in Atlanta.

When Vine was founded in 2012, its creators—Dom Hofmann, Rus Yusupov, and Colin Kroll—never thought about it being a way to launch careers. They were simply looking to create a utility that made it easier for people to splice together and share videos electronically (because video files had been too huge to share via text message or email). "We wanted to build a tool that would easily cut video shots together. That's really all it was," Hofmann told *Wired*. Then, seemingly overnight, Vine became *the* video-sharing app.

Consider this: In 2012, Vine was released to the public. Just four months later, Twitter bought it for the tidy sum of $30 million. A good value, it turns out, because by 2015, users were watching Vines at a rate of 1 billion *per day*. The app had 200 million active users streaming Vine videos each month. And of that user base, 71 percent were millennials. So in that sense, it's not surprising that the medium (with an assist from some other social media sites, of course) has catapulted Shawn to superstardom.

Turns out Shawn had been watching cover videos for years, before Vine

---

Heard It Through the (Great) Vine

"DON'T"
MAY 11, 2014

Covering one of his favorite artists, Ed Sheeran, Shawn did an acoustic version of Sheeran's breakup dis.

"LET IT GO"
APRIL 21, 2014

Shawn did a red-hot version of Disney's Frozen *anthem.*

---

was even invented. Like a lot of kids, he watched his fair share of YouTube. "I was super obsessed.... When I was like 10 I would come home from school and watch them from four o'clock until eight o'clock every night," he told *Entertainment Weekly*. "I was so intrigued that people took these super popular songs and did them their own way. It really showed me the creativity, how every person sang it their own way and even how they would film and record it."

Shawn's own Internet debut all started back in 2012. No, not on Vine but on, yes, YouTube! He has a few full and partial covers on YouTube that show early promise, including versions of Adele, Hunter Hayes, and Rihanna songs. (How's *that* for variety?) But he wasn't a very active YouTuber.

He began Vining in the spring of 2013 when he started posting videos he shot with his friends. The very first of them *had* to have been experimental. It features Shawn in the darkness, backlit by only a sunny window and tagged "my #firstpost on Vine." And indeed, that's what Vine is for many users: a window into a person's life.

Heard It Through the (Great) Vine

"COMPLICATED"
APRIL 15, 2014

We're not frustrated listening to Shawn go old-school on fellow Canadian Avril Lavigne's ballad.

"SUMMERTIME SADNESS"
MARCH 17, 2014

Shawn has called Lana Del Rey's brooding song one of his all-time favorites to cover.

" Vine was the perfect platform because no one else was doing it. "

The "Life of the Party" himself.

Shawn performs at New York City's Hammerstein Ballroom in 2014. A year and a half later, he would sell out Radio City Music Hall.

Shawn's early Vines show off his playful side. He and his buddies play pranks on one another, goof off at school, hang out at the beach, go swimming, joke with their families. In one Vine he lets a friendly squirrel climb on him. In another, he performs strongman feats with a prop yardstick. He clowns around shooting hoops and making silly faces into the camera. The Shawn we see is anything but serious or brooding or even ambitious—he's just a normal kid who loves his family and friends and doesn't take himself too seriously. In other words, he's the same Shawn legions of fans love today.

The first time Shawn sang on Vine was back in June 2013—making up funny songs about his friends! And even though he's known for that Bieber cover, his first-ever cover was actually *very* different. He chose a song by the gone-but-not-forgotten songstress Amy Winehouse, a bonus track

Heard It Through the (Great) Vine

"ALL OF ME"
JANUARY 29, 2014

Shawn and John Legend: the perfect combination!

"DARK HORSE"
JANUARY 12, 2014

Pop princess Katy Perry's hit got a new spin with Shawn's acoustic cover.

Heard It Through the (Great) Vine

"STORY OF MY LIFE"
NOVEMBER 5, 2013

Clash of the dreamboats! Shawn covers 1D and Vine swoons.

"WONDERWALL"
OCTOBER 26, 2013

Shawn loops a video of himself covering the Oasis classic in front of a Toronto audience.

on the deluxe edition of her 2006 album *Back to Black* called "Valerie." The song itself is a sad one, mourning a relationship lost to addiction, but the song gets a little lilt from its reggae-inspired beat. Perhaps that's what attracted Shawn to it (remember, Shawn inherited a love of reggae from his parents).

As time went on, Shawn started to polish his Internet form. He watched YouTube videos and Vines and saw what worked and what didn't. He looked for interesting songs and taught himself how to play the melodies on guitar. He experimented with vocal styles, sometimes posting back-to-back variations on the same tune. In short, he was honing his craft.

An active Viner through the spring and summer of 2013, Shawn received a pretty big shock at the end of July, just a week or so before his 15th birthday. It was seemingly just another Vine—Shawn sitting in his bedroom, strumming the guitar and singing yet another pop song. Cut, uploaded, and live. Except this time...people noticed.

"I woke up in the morning and looked on my Vine and I had 10,000 followers. It was

fanchat

"If it weren't for this insanely talented kid...I don't know where I would be today[.] his music and encouraging words have helped me [through] the some of the absolute hardest times of my life"

—@lilmuffinmendes via Twitter

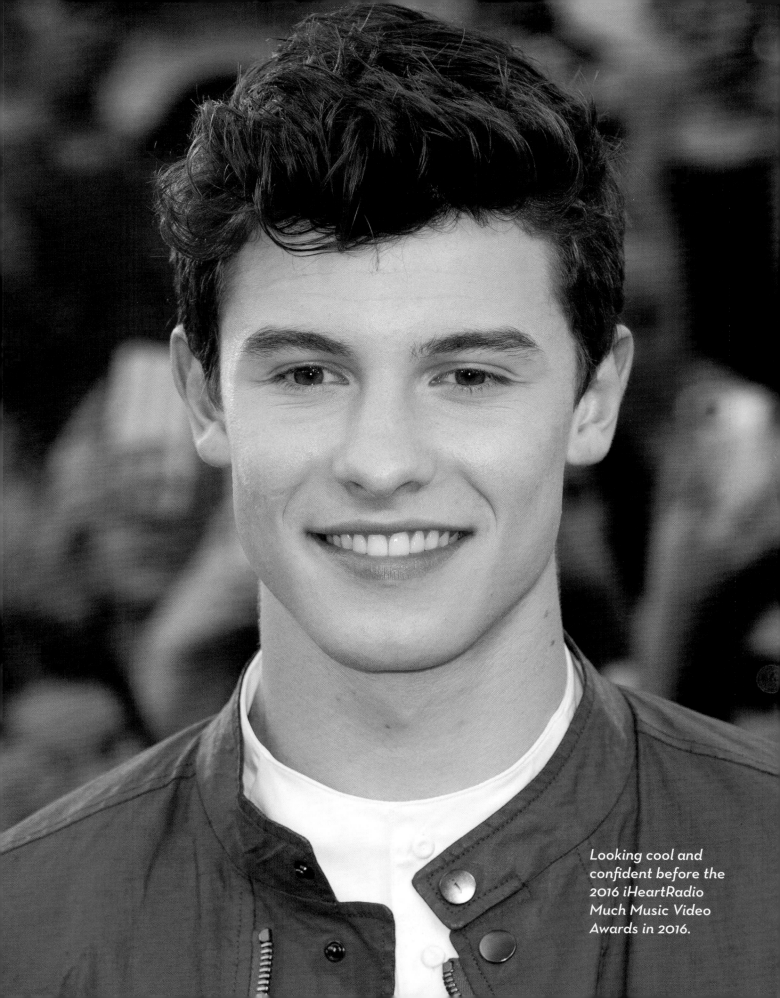

Looking cool and confident before the 2016 iHeartRadio Much Music Video Awards in 2016.

Rock on! Shawn gets silly at the 2015 Much Music Video Awards.

just an explosion," he told *Entertainment Weekly*. "I was overwhelmed and didn't even really know what was going on. All I could do was post another one, and it was the same deal, and from there on it was a snowball effect."

Shawn was stunned by the sudden attention. "When I put that first Vine out, I was just doing it for fun; there was no wanting to become an artist," he told the *New York Times*. "But then when I realized the potential it had, I thought Vine was the perfect platform because no one else was doing it. I would have been one of the only ones, or one of the first."

He was quick to reach out to his fans, responding just a day later. "Honestly the biggest thank-you to everyone who's liked or vined my last two Vines and followed me," he posted. And indeed his fans started watching, revining, and telling all their friends. Soon, 10,000 became 20,000...and 50,000. (Perhaps it's this overnight success that inspired Shawn's single "Something Big." Consider the chorus: *Something big I feel it happening / Out of my control / Pushing, pulling, and*

Heard It Through the (Great) Vine

"RADIOACTIVE"
SEPTEMBER 14, 2013

Shawn tapped the indie rockers Imagine Dragons for a rooftop serenade.

"THE A TEAM"
AUGUST 22, 2013

Sheeran's first hit was prime pickings for a remake.

---

it's grabbing me / Feel it in my bones. Just sayin'!)

He'd fashion musical messages to his fans, riffing ditties like "The sun is out and I'm feeling okay. / I hope you have a really good day." He began cross-promoting on his Twitter, Instagram, YouTube, and Facebook accounts. He interacted with his fans and followers directly, fielding questions and answering requests. It was, and remains, a true back-and-forth.

There's no denying Shawn's ability to remain authentic is what's kept him popular with fans. He doesn't forget how he got to the top. "One of the biggest things is staying in contact with my fans—very intimate contact," he told Fuse TV. "If I let people take over my Twitter and talk to the fans themselves...you don't have that strength that I have between them. I'm just literally asking them questions and DMing them."

Then he came up with an idea. "Hey, how many of you guys would come to a concert of mine if I did one in Toronto?" he posted on October 7, 2013. The response was immediate and enthusiastic, and he made arrangements to do a live show a few weeks later to a huge crowd. (You can see footage from that very first show on his Vine account—aww!)

He started playing out more frequently—a pop-up here, a small venue there—and people started showing up in droves. Less than a year after his first Vine cover went live, he was playing his own music at a pop-up show in New

York City's Times Square to several hundred. And two years after that, he sold out Radio City Music Hall. He played Madison Square Garden in September.

As of this writing, Shawn has 4.8 million followers on Vine, 7.3 million on Twitter, 12.8 million on Instagram, and 4.7 million likes on Facebook. But those numbers keep climbing and climbing. It seems there's only one way for Shawn to go these days: up! ★

Heard It Through the (Great) Vine

"AS LONG AS YOU LOVE ME"
JULY 28, 2013

The Vine heard 'round the world? Shawn got a huge boost from this Biebs song.

"WHEN I WAS YOUR MAN"
JULY 28, 2013

Singing Bruno Mars, Shawn makes his followers wish he was their man! (And yes, that's sis Aaliyah in the background.)

Shawn takes the stage solo in New Jersey in 2015.

The MAGCON Family

Chapter Four:
The MAGCON Family

Bart Bordelon might not have been the first one to recognize the potential that a tour of Internet-famous personalities could have, but he was certainly the first to act on it. It was September 2013, and Bordelon, a single dad and start-up entrepreneur from Shreveport, Louisiana, was just another parent scratching his head about his kids' latest flavor of the month. As it turned out, he was a family friend of Aaron Carpenter, then an Internet celebrity with more than 200,000 Twitter followers. Carpenter had casually mentioned to his Instagram followers that he was meeting with a few fans at a Dallas shopping mall, and hundreds showed up, causing pandemonium.

"My thought was, if I brought a bunch of guys together and we organized it, made it more of a formal event, made it a party, made it fun for the fans, this thing could go big," Bordelon, father of five, said in 2014. With Carpenter the first on board, MAGCON was born.

The first MAGCON brought together 10 individuals of varying talents, from musicians to DJs to humorous vloggers. All of them were fresh successes on the growing video-sharing app Vine (in addition to their other outlets of social media expression, because nobody can choose just one!). Among them was a fresh-faced 15-year-old from Pickering, Ontario.

MAGCON, for the uninitiated, stands for meet-and-greet convention. It was, as Bordelon likes to call it, "a boy-band phenomenon without the band." Fans could buy tickets to see their favorite social media stars in the flesh, and VIPs could even talk to the boys one-on-one. All the while, the MAGCONners were vining the events, putting the fans smack-dab in the middle of the action.

VOCABULARY LESSON

newborn \\'n(y)ü -'bȯ(ə)rn

A recent fan of the MAGCON Family; someone who has not been around since the beginning.

Perfecting his onstage style in 2015.

Greeting the press at the US Open in 2014.

It was a brilliant conceit that gave fans unprecedented access to the celebrities they followed on social media.

Social media is a pretty intimate medium, and the distance between a Viner and the screen is incredibly small. As a result, many fans already felt they knew their favorite Vine celeb and what made him tick. Getting to meet him in person was just the icing on the cake. These guys weren't hard to reach like, say, a certain pop star. When asked by Gawker what made the MAGCONners so special, one fan said, "They're actually our age, and we can meet them." Said another, "They're better than Justin

PARTY IN THE USA

The MAGCON Family made eight stops on their first nationwide tour: Houston, Dallas, Orlando, Washington, DC, Nashville, Chicago, San Diego, and San Francisco.

WE ARE FAMILY

The participants who make up the MAGCON tour generally refer to themselves as the MAGCON Family. Many of them remain close after the tours are over.

Bieber. There's more of them, so no one has to share."

From the beginning, the MAGCON tour was a huge success, selling thousands of tickets at every tour stop across the country. Fans—and their parents—flocked to venues from San Diego to Orlando to our nation's capital. A date in Chicago sold out in 30 seconds. The massive following stunned even Bordelon, who knew he had lightning in a bottle.

So what *did* a MAGCON event look like? For starters, there was nothing "conventional" about them. Each six-hour event was presided over by a DJ (Mahogany LOX, most usually), while the guys stood around and chatted informally

Chapter Four:
The MAGCON Family

with fans, performed small skits, or told jokes. It was in this environment that Shawn's talent started to stand out. For many of his tourmates, whose success was distilled to silly six-second clips like making fun of self-conscious selfies or gyrating to hip-hop music, the larger stage and longer time frame didn't work as well. It's easy to be funny for a moment, but filling a bigger expanse was more challenging. By contrast, Shawn was able to showcase his talents as a singer and performer. Performing a full set of cover songs (with tunes including favorites from Ed Sheeran to Lana Del Rey), Shawn got to show a greater range of his vocal abilities. It was a golden opportunity for him to further polish his onstage skills, as well as his fan engagement.

But, like the cliché goes, all good things must come to an end. Just two years after MAGCON took the world by storm, the tour disintegrated. Bordelon reflected on the short-lived phenomenon with bittersweetness. "It's like the '92 Olympic basketball team, the Dream Team," he told Vulture.

A portrait of the singer-songwriter in 2014.

"That will never be duplicated. That's once in a lifetime."

Fans were stunned and shocked, posting grief-stricken messages on social media and even resorting to self-harm. In a sad footnote to MAGCON, the hashtag #cutforMAGCON was a trending topic when news broke that the tour had dissolved.

The show has regrouped and continues today under different management, but it doesn't come anywhere close to capturing the magic of those original dates. So far, Shawn excepted, none of the MAGCON boys have transcended their online success to other arenas, though most of them are still working at it, staying active on social media. Keep your eyes peeled and you'll see some of your favorite original MAGCONners making appearances on movies and TV.

It's a credit to Shawn and his talent as a musician that he's been able to translate his Vine following into something big. Just months after embarking on the MAGCON tour, he was cutting an album with Island Records, hooking on to tours with Austin Mahone and Taylor Swift, and poised for something big—something even bigger than he had ever expected. ★

fanchat

"SHAWN OMFG GAHHHH ZAAYYY YUUUMMM BAE I LOVE YOU #Magcon Tour"

—Sesha Patel via Pinterest

THE ORIGINAL MAGCON FAMILY

Aaron Carpenter
The one who started it all, Twitter celeb Aaron Carpenter was just 15 when MAGCON began.

Nash Grier
This North Carolinian found Vine fame six humorous seconds at a time.

Cameron Dallas
Initially the biggest name of the lineup, "Cam" Dallas remains one of the world's most famous social media stars.

Taylor Caniff
The indisputable bad boy of the MAGCONners, the singer has recently had trouble with the law.

Jack Gilinsky and Jack Johnson
Known to the masses as Jack & Jack, they have a signature blend of music and comedy.

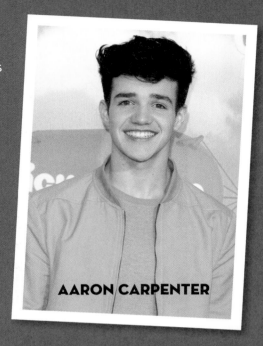
AARON CARPENTER

CAMERON DALLAS

NASH GRIER

Matthew Espinosa
This Bieber lookalike got Vine-famous posting fun facts about himself.

Carter Reynolds
Another humorous vlogger, he's been called a "king of self-promotion" and got his plea for more followers, #carterto200K, to trend nationally.

Shawn Mendes
Need we say more?

DJ Mahogany LOX
MAGCON's only female artist and unofficial mascot, she is the granddaughter of Motown founder Berry Gordy.

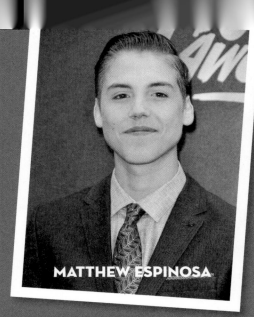
MATTHEW ESPINOSA

JACK & JACK

MAHOGANY LOX

CHAPTER FIVE

Something Big

Shawn strikes a bashful pose onstage at the Greek Theatre in Los Angeles in 2015.

Chapter Five:
Something Big

If everything up to that point had felt like an overnight success—the Vine numbers, the wild ride of the MAGCON tour—then what happened next must have been even more shocking.

In May 2014 Shawn got a phone call that would change his life. Andrew Gertler, an up-and-coming talent scout and manager, happened upon a YouTube clip of Shawn belting out A Great Big World's "Say Something." It was a song the executive had heard recently that he thought would be a great song for cover artists to tackle because of its emotional weight and vocal range. He went searching for versions of it online and came across Shawn's.

Gertler saw Shawn's video and stopped in his tracks. "I actually didn't even know about his big Vine following, it was more so just his pure talent that struck me and

DID YOU KNOW?

Manager Andrew Gertler is only nine years older than Shawn!

caused me to reach out immediately," he told All Access. After a couple weeks of near-constant badgering, he convinced Shawn and his family to fly out to New York to talk further about Shawn's future, record some music, and meet with some record labels.

From then on, it all snowballed. "Island Records was the first record label to... acknowledge me," Shawn told *Billboard*. "After that, quickly Republic Records, and then Atlantic Records, Sony Records and Warner Bros. It was all the labels at once. It was absolutely insane...knowing that this many record labels were interested in me." To say he was flattered is an understatement.

"He had written a bunch of songs on his own," Gertler told *Rolling Stone*. "From the very beginning, he was set on the fact that he was going to write his own music and that he was a songwriter.

JUNE 4, 2014

THIS DAY IN SHAWN-STORY

Shawn signs with Island Records. Life as he knows it changes forever!

Chapter Five:
Something Big

When we heard some of these songs, everyone's ears perked up. He was so naturally talented."

Island won out, in part because they saw Shawn for the artist he wanted to become. Some might have seen him as the next Bieber—an Internet star-turned-pop confection—but Island Records head Ziggy Chareton felt otherwise. "I take no offense to [comparisons between Shawn and Bieber] because [Bieber] became extremely successful, but the one thing I will say about Shawn is you're never going to see him onstage with 30 background dancers, pyrotechnics, and records produced and having features from Nicki Minaj," Chareton told *Billboard*.

With a label deal inked, Shawn began to define his sound. Using John Mayer, Ed Sheeran, and the group One Republic as touch points, he started working on songs for an upcoming EP. Meanwhile, he started performing again, joining Austin Mahone's nationwide tour as an opening act. While on the road with Mahone, he released *The Shawn Mendes EP*, which includes the single "Life of the Party," among others. The tour was a good incubator for his new material, and many of the Mahomies were familiar with Shawn from his previous showcases on Vine and with MAGCON.

Shawn joined Mahone, British rockers the Vamps, and Fifth Harmony for Austin Mahone: Live on Tour, a 30-city swing

fanchat
"I really love Shawn because I think he's an incredibly talented individual with a really big heart! :)"

—throwbackmendes on Tumblr

Shawn brings the drama in a 2016 performance.

Shawn gives good face in Berlin.

through the United States (with a pit stop in Toronto, Shawn's hometown!). Mahone gave his fan base a backstage pass into life on tour, posting webisodes of Austin Mahone #TourLife on YouTube. Some of the videos show the audiences, giving an indication of just how big the stage had gotten for Shawn. Others show what the stars end up doing in their downtime. Unsurprisingly, Shawn is often found sitting around strumming a guitar. In between there are funny and sincere moments depicting life on the road. The vignettes are just another peek into the life of a guy who already shares so much with his fans via social media.

In November 2014, just weeks after Shawn wrapped up with Mahone, Taylor Swift took to her website to announce the hotly anticipated opening acts to her upcoming *1989* world tour. Joining her for the first leg of the tour, through North America, would be Australian footballer–turned–singer-songwriter Vance Joy and Vine cover artist–turned–singer-songwriter Shawn.

Shawn poses with Austin Mahone tourmates the Vamps at BBC Radio's Teen Awards in 2014.

Chapter Five:
Something Big

Mendes broke the news to his Twitter followers that same day, complete with heart-eyed and cheering emoticons. He was psyched!

Days later, he was still shell-shocked. "I cant really think about it because by the time it gets there I'll start getting excited," he told MTV. "I will have to pinch myself every day when I'm on that tour. She's Taylor Swift. It's crazy."

Joining Swift on tour was "almost like as a kid when you try out for a rec soccer team or hockey team and you get the call like you made the team. I had that same exact feeling," he continued. More like a baseball player being called up to the majors. This, undeniably, was the big time. Gone were the small venues and arenas;

he would literally be playing in major league ballparks and pro football stadiums across the continent.

Swift's North American tour stormed into Toronto on October 2 for the first of two sold-out shows, and newbie Shawn was the first to take the stage before the massive crowd in the Rogers Centre. The *Toronto Star*, reviewing the concert, gave him a rave review: "If opening act Shawn Mendes was even the slightest bit daunted about playing in front of 45,000 people with his acoustic guitar as his only crutch, the Pickering resident didn't show it…. Handling himself with great poise, confidence, and humility, Mendes has a long, healthy career in front of him."

Given his success with Swift, it was inevitable that Shawn would start headlining eventually. In between dates with Taylor, Shawn did solo shows in the fall of 2014 in New York, Los Angeles, Chicago, and Toronto. All four of them sold out *within minutes*.

The dates with Taylor, which wrapped up in late 2015, gave Shawn a huge boost in profile and chart performance. Night after night of performing to huge crowds

DID YOU KNOW?

Taylor Swift called Shawn onstage during her set in Seattle, leading the crowd of 55,000 in a rendition of "Happy Birthday to You" to commemorate Shawn's big 1-7!

Shawn greets fans on Rockefeller Plaza at Today.
Some fans camped out overnight to see him!

also cemented his onstage confidence. So in early 2016 he announced 38 dates for *his own* world tour (a few more were added later, including a sold-out-in-seconds opening night at the iconic Radio City Music Hall in New York). Fans answered the call, and the entire tour sold out in six minutes. The tour includes dates through North America, as well as a monthlong European leg.

It's a lot to put on the shoulders of a kid who just turned 18, but so far Shawn has proved himself more than up for the task. "The way I keep myself sane is by thinking of it as fun," he told *Forbes*, which named him among their *30 Under 30* in music in 2016. And from the looks of it, it's hard to tell who's having more fun: Shawn, or the legion of fans who comprise the Mendes Army. ★

TAYLOR'S GREATEST HITS

Shawn is just one of the many artists to have opened for Taylor Swift before going on to bigger successes. Here are a few more artists who have joined the squad over the years.

ED SHEERAN

Ed Sheeran

British singer-songwriter Sheeran joined Taylor on the North American leg of her Red tour in 2013.

HAIM

HAIM

This sister act rocked out several dates on the 1989 tour.

AUSTIN MAHONE

Austin Mahone

Yep, Swifty was an original Mahomie.

Florida Georgia Line

This award-winning country duo got a huge boost from Swift's Red tour.

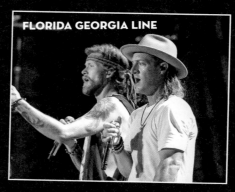
FLORIDA GEORGIA LINE

Brett Eldredge

The "Don't Ya" singer's debut album went gold after touring with Tay-Tay.

BRETT ELDREDGE

James Bay

The British singer-songwriter, and part-time 1989 tourmate, was nominated for a Best New Artist Grammy in 2016.

JAMES BAY

WHERE IN THE WORLD IS SHAWN?

Seems like these days, he's everywhere. From the beginning of the MAGCON tour to opening for Austin Mahone and Taylor Swift, Shawn has been on the road constantly. He started his own world tour in March 2016 at Radio City Music Hall and has been on the move ever since. Did you see him in your town?:

March 5	New York, New York
March 6	Houston, Texas
March 19	Orlando, Florida
April 16	Cologne, Germany
April 17	Amsterdam, the Netherlands
April 19	Frederiksburg, Denmark
April 21	Stockholm, Sweden
April 22	Oslo, Norway
April 24	Berlin, Germany
April 27	Milan, Italy
April 29	Madrid, Spain
May 2	Paris, France
May 5 & 6	London, United Kingdom
May 8	Lisbon, Portugal
July 15	Boca Raton, Florida

July 16	St. Augustine, Florida
July 17	Atlanta, Georgia
July 19	San Antonio, Texas
July 20	Grand Prairie, Texas
July 22	Phoenix, Arizona
July 23	San Diego, California
July 24	San Jose, California
July 26	Seattle, Washington
July 27	Vancouver, British Columbia
July 30	Salt Lake City, Utah
July 31	Broomfield, Colorado
August 2	St. Paul, Minnesota
August 4	West Allis, Wisconsin
August 5	Rosemont, Illinois
August 6	St. Louis, Missouri
August 7	Nashville, Tennessee
August 10	Detroit, Michigan
August 12	Baltimore, Maryland
August 13	Hamburg, New York
August 14	Philadelphia, Pennsylvania
August 16	West Long Branch, New Jersey
August 17	Lowell, Massachusetts
August 19	Uncasville, Connecticut
August 20	Hershey, Pennsylvania
August 21	Toronto, Ontario
September 10	New York, NY

Giving Back

Chapter Six:
Giving Back

It's clear from Shawn's music that he has a big heart. Which is why it's no surprise that besides being a songwriter who composes beautiful songs about love and heartbreak and inspiration that help people overcome their own obstacles, he's also a person who dedicates his time and energy to those less fortunate than him.

Doing charity work isn't something he has to do, it's something he wants to do. In the short time Shawn has been in the spotlight, he's lent his talents and energy to a number of charitable causes.

In 2014, he joined Jessie J and Nick Jonas as one of the featured artists in the 15th anniversary fund-raiser for Musicians

On Call, a foundation that brings the healing power of music, through live and recorded performances, to the bedsides of patients across the country. Since its 1999 inception, Musicians On Call performers have visited more than half a million patients. The 2014 benefit concert raised more than $700,000 for the foundation, which underscores the healing power of music. Later in 2014, Shawn performed at the Z100's Jingle Ball in New York City, which raised money and awareness for the Ryan Seacrest Foundation, aiding pediatric hospitals nationwide.

He also joined forces with the Salvation Army for Rock the Red Kettle, performing in the organization's benefit concert. And he took to social media to galvanize his fan base. "I've been really inspired by the work the Salvation Army does to help kids who need a safe place to sleep, a meal and a place to hang out after school," Shawn told his followers. "I hope my fans will help me give back this season and will also help spread the spirit of giving by posting their own #RedKettleReasons."

He also partnered with the Grammy Foundation to create awareness for

DID YOU KNOW?

Music really does heal! Studies have shown that exposure to music lowers blood pressure, helps with pain management, reduces stress and alters mood, assists Alzheimer's patients in recalling the past, and ameliorates Parkinson's disease, among many other ailments.

Shawn joins fellow recording artists for Musicians On Call's 15th Anniversary Celebration in 2014.

Shawn performs at the 2014 Z100 Jingle Ball in New York City.

struggling music and arts programs in schools. Through contributing a small donation to music education efforts, fans entered to win a VIP experience with Shawn, including plane and concert tickets, backstage access, and a personal hangout with Shawn himself! "I think everybody deserves a chance to learn what they want to learn," he told fans online in his appeal for music education.

In 2015 he focused efforts on bringing education to those less fortunate. Partnering with Pencils of Promise, a nonprofit organization that focuses on building education infrastructure in underdeveloped areas, he launched a campaign to #BuildASchoolWithShawn.

The effort met its fund-raising goal after just one social media post, and contributors saw their donations become a school in rural Ghana. "I'm so excited we were able to raise enough funds to build a school for the kids in Shia, Ghana," said Shawn. "This means the world to me."

He also participated as a performer in WE Day, "a celebration of youth making a difference in their local and global communities," as described on WE.org. "WE Day brings together world-renowned speakers and award-winning performers with tens of thousands of young people to celebrate their contributions and kick-start another year of change." The first WE Day started in Canada in 2008. Since then, the

fanchat

"#NotesFromShawn is the sweetest thing I've ever done !!...it really spreads joy !!"

—@nemrahsaquib via Twitter

Spreading joy is Shawn's stock in trade.

event has grown to 14 locations across the globe. More important, the WE movement is growing. More than 200,000 students, all of whom are affecting change in their communities and around the world, attended WE Day events last year.

But no cause is more important to Shawn than his own charity, which targets a cause extremely important to him: stopping bullying. He saw his own fans crying out on social media. He observed people coming to his shows with cutting marks. He saw the nasty Internet comments and how quickly negativity could spread.

In 2015, he partnered with DoSomething.org to create a campaign called Notes from Shawn and inject a little *positivity* into the mix. The effort

DID YOU KNOW?

You can't buy a ticket to WE Day. Students earn their event tickets by taking one local and one global action through WE Schools, our yearlong educational program that engages and empowers young people to become compassionate leaders and active citizens. Some students collect food for homeless shelters. Others raise money to build classrooms overseas. Every young person makes their own journey to WE Day, but together, they discover their power to change the world.

—From WE.org

"[My desire to help others comes from] wanting to do that [as an individual], but it also comes from having a great opportunity to be able to make a difference and help motivate because it's easier for me than it would be for your average 17-year-old, who doesn't have as big of a voice as me."

Chapter Six:
Giving Back

was inspired by his song "Life of the Party," which focuses on self-esteem and feelings of depression. DoSomething. org, a charitable website that focuses specifically on galvanizing social change and volunteerism in young people, was the perfect foil. "About 40% of young people have experienced self-harm or know someone who has. One major cause of that is low self-esteem," the website reports. "Shawn Mendes is on a world tour and a mission to spread positivity and joy around the globe. Join him! Do your part by secretly posting encouraging notes that will give self-esteem boosts to everyone who sees them!"

"The campaign was called Notes from Shawn. All I was asking my fans to do was get a sticky note and write 'You rock' or 'You're amazing,' just something to make someone's day," Shawn told *Samaritan* magazine. "And I did it too; I put sticky

Fans flocked to New York City to see Shawn give a free concert in June 2016.

Performing at WE Day 2015 in London.

notes all over while I was touring across America."

The notes are posted anonymously and the recipient is oftentimes random. The idea being that everyone matters, every life counts. "You are beautiful." "Use your voice." "Smile more. It looks good on you." "I promise you, it does not rain forever." These are just a few of the multitude of notes Shawn has inspired.

To this day, #NotesFromShawn endures online and in posts across social media, as well as out there in the real world. The notes are testimonials to the thousands upon thousands of days he's brightened. "It was really truly incredible the fact that we had 60,000 people sign up [initially]," he continued. "If you go online and type in 'handwritten notes from Shawn,' you'll see millions of pictures."

DID YOU KNOW?

The Salvation Army provides nearly 60 million meals and 10 million nights of shelter each year.

DID YOU KNOW?

Since its inception, Pencils of Promise has built more than 300 schools and educated more than 30,000 students.

In fact, the campaign has been so successful that he's recently combined efforts with the Paper Mate company to #SpreadJoy. The office supply company issued a series of pens promoting the positive message, and the notes of encouragement, compassion, and, yes, joy continue to proliferate. Now *that's* doing something!

It's no surprise, given Shawn's outreach efforts and his ability to inspire others, that *Time* magazine has named him one of its Most Influential Teens for two years running, alongside such trailblazers as Jazz Jennings, Malala Yousafzai, Malia and Sasha Obama, and Kylie and Kendall Jenner.

As evidenced by Notes from Shawn, he's not afraid to tackle Internet bullies head-on. ★

By writing Notes from Shawn, "we can make someone a little happier together," Shawn Instagrammed

DON'T STOP THE MUSIC!

According to the grassroots fund-raising website DoSomething.org, here are 10 very good reasons to support music educations in schools.

1. Children who study music tend to have larger vocabularies and more advanced reading skills than their peers who do not participate in music lessons.

2. Children with learning disabilities or dyslexia who tend to lose focus with more noise could benefit greatly from music lessons.

3. Music programs are constantly in danger of being cut from shrinking school budgets even though they're proven to improve academics.

4. Children who study a musical instrument are more likely to excel in all of their studies, work better in teams, have enhanced critical thinking skills, stay in school, and pursue further education.

5. In the past, secondary students who participated in a music group at school reported the lowest lifetime and current use of all substances (tobacco, alcohol, and illicit drugs).

6. Schools with music programs have an estimated 90.2% graduation rate and 93.9% attendance rate compared to schools without music education, which average 72.9% graduation and 84.9% attendance.

7. Regardless of socioeconomic status or school district, students (3rd graders) who participate in high-quality music programs score higher on reading and spelling tests.

8. A Stanford study shows that music engages areas of the brain which are involved with paying attention, making predictions and updating events in our memory.

9. Much like expert technical skills, mastery in arts and humanities is closely correlated to a greater understanding of language components.

10. Young children who take music lessons show different brain development and improved memory over the course of a year, compared to children who do not receive musical training.

—FROM DOSOMETHING.ORG

Shawn performs his inspirational song "Life of the Party" at the 2015 Juno Awards.

Success Is "Handwritten"

Performing tracks from Handwritten at the Much Music Video Awards.

It wasn't so long ago that Shawn was just another kid sitting at home watching YouTube videos of his favorite artists doing their thing. And it wasn't that long ago that he picked up a guitar and starting strumming along with them, belting out the lyrics along with Ed and John and Adele and Amy and the rest of them.

He got his first guitar at 15 and, inspired by the craft of his favorite musicians, started teaching himself how to play by watching those videos. He studied the artists' vocalizations, the choices they made stylistically. He analyzed how different singers tackled the same song, and started to develop his own critical ear for tackling songs himself. Thus began a musical odyssey that started innocently enough—Mendes posting videos online of himself singing the pop hits of the day— and became something big indeed.

So in 2015, with MAGCON behind him and on tour with Austin Mahone, Shawn set his sights on bigger things. He found time to write and record a full-length album all while on the road. Believe it or not, all 12 singles—10 of 12 of which were cowritten by Shawn—were recorded on a tour bus!

INKED

In celebration of the success of Handwritten, and as a reminder of the things that matter most to him, Shawn got his first tattoo in June 2016, just two months before his 18th birthday. At first glance, it looks like the Toronto landscape, with the CN Tower and woods looming over Lake Ontario. Zoom out and you'll see the whole thing is in the shape of a guitar. And look closely at the bridge of the guitar: that's actually a sound wave (a recording of his family saying "I love you").

Even before its official release, *Handwritten* had a terrific pedigree. Its first single, "Life of the Party" (which was also featured on *The Shawn Mendes EP*), made him the youngest artist to crack the Billboard Top 25 with a debut single.

"I put so much hard work into this and am so excited to share it with the world! It really is true to who I am as a writer and artist," Shawn told his fans about the album in 2015. And they responded en masse. By the end of the first week of its release, *Handwritten* had sold 119,000 copies and was the #1 album in the US.

In a way, Shawn is rewriting the rules for album promotion in the ever-changing landscape of the music industry. Leading up to the release of *Handwritten*, he teased sound bites and tidbits from the album to his fans and followers. He counted down the days to its release, urging fans to help him break sales records for preorders and downloads. And he leveraged his platform as a social media sensation perhaps more than any artist before him.

Rather than relying on radio play, he communicated with fans directly through social media. "From his very first single ever breaking into the Hot 100's Top 25 with absolutely zero radio play to now having a No. 1 album, it's all off of the strength of Shawn and the connection he has with his fans," manager Andrew Gertler told Mashable. "We put them in the driver's seat, and let them share in the success—because it really is their success story, not just ours."

Shawn initially didn't want to include songs on the album that he didn't have a hand in writing, but when he heard

fanchat

"I love Shawn! I think he is really good at what he does and it must take him a long time to write his songs. My favorite songs are 'Stitches' and 'Something Big.' They both have a lot of action in them."

—George Dunnick, Age 7, Chicago

Proving his star shines bright in 2015.

the demo for "Stitches," he "fell in love." It turns out Shawn had good instincts. When released in November 2015, the fourth single trailing "Life of the Party," "Something Big," and "A Little Too Much," it smashed forecasted predictions, spending 22 weeks on the Billboard chart and peaking at #4. Long gone were the days of no radio support. "Stitches" was a #1-charting radio hit and went quadruple platinum.

The tracks on *Handwritten* range from danceable anthems like "Stitches" and "Something Big" to beautiful ballads like "Never Be Alone" and "Crazy." Unsurprisingly, the unifying theme in many of them is love. "I think love is the strongest human emotion and one of the

NAME THAT TUNE

Can you match the lyric to the track? Keep an eye on the clock to see how you rate as a Mendes matcher.

Got a feeling that I'm going under   "Something Big"

Yell so loud, won't forget our names   "Aftertaste"

Am I just hanging on to all the words she used to say? "Ruin"

I'm permanent, you can't erase me   "Stitches"

Take your shot, it might be scary   "The Weight"

Do you...do you think about me?   "I Know What You Did Last Summer"

When you try to take me back my heavy heart just breaks "Treat You Better"

I'll stop time for you the second you say you'd like me to "Life of the Party"

30 seconds or less: Congratulations, you're general of the Mendes Army!
30 seconds to 1 minute: Not bad. Not bad at all.
More than 1 minute: Time to go back for another listen.

most fun and easiest things to write about. It was always really fun to write a love song," Shawn told the *Toronto Sun*.

So how does he come up with the stuff of his songs, then? It turns out, inspiration is not only in the most predictable places, but everywhere. "My inspiration literally comes from everything, however random or specific; there's no one specific thing," he told MTV UK.

"I used to write stories. Handwriting stories in school [was] a big deal for me," he told Digital Spy. And like any good craftsman, his skills have matured over time. When asked if his songwriting style has changed since he started the process,

IN THE MOOD FOR MENDES

Here's the perfect playlist of Shawn's tunes, for whatever mood you might be in!

If you're feeling...	Then play...
All alone	"A Little Too Much"
Anxious about tomorrow's test	"Something Big"
Bent on revenge	"I Know What You Did Last Summer"
Bursting with emotions	"Ruin"
Butterflies	"Kid in Love"
Invincible	"Show You"
Like getting back together might be a good idea	"Bring It Back"
Like it might be over	"Three Empty Words"
Like you're stuck in the friend zone	"Strings"
Ready for an adventure	"One of Those Nights"
So not over your breakup	"Stitches"
Up for anything	"Lost"

Shawn delights fans in Spain on his 2016 world tour.

Shawn visits The Jonathan
Ross Show *in London.*

he continued, "Every time I write a song my approach changes. I feel like every time I write a song it feels like the first time I wrote a song. It's just as hard, it doesn't get easier but that's why I love it: because it's a challenge every time. I also feel like I'm learning new ways."

The success of the album was a huge boost for the first-time songwriter. He was learning to trust his abilities and building confidence as a writer and musician. And then, something happened out of the blue. On tour with Taylor Swift, Shawn ran into acquaintance and former Austin Mahone tourmate Camila Cabello of Fifth Harmony. "We were just backstage. There were like 100 people in my dressing room at the time, and it was madness back there, but I had this guitar and I was just jamming out," he said. "And we basically wrote a pre-chorus and a chorus in like 30 minutes." That jam session ultimately became the blistering cheating duet "I Know What You Did Last Summer."

The off-the-cuff single was certified platinum, and peaked at #20 on the Billboard charts. It also led to a swirl of rumors about the dating status of the two performers, who consistently deflected allegations that they were an item. "Can I be honest? I don't believe you," *The Late Late Show* host James Corden told the pair when they (yet again) denied having a romantic connection. "I don't care," replied Shawn.

Just for the record, the two aren't dating. And the song "I Know What You Did Last Summer" is actually about some sleazeball that *X Factor* alum Cabello actually did date before she found out he was flirting with another friend of hers. Romantic entanglements aside, Shawn still has plenty of admiration for his duet partner. "She's phenomenal," he told *Seventeen*. "I love

> ## RECORD BREAKER
>
> *Technically, the youngest artist ever to appear on the Billboard charts is Blue Ivy Carter. The daughter of Jay-Z and Beyoncé was credited on her famous daddy's track "Glory," which cracked the charts in January 2012, just two days after her birth.*

Chapter Seven:
Success Is "Handwritten"

DID **YOU** KNOW?

Shawn and Camila Cabello weren't friends on the Austin Mahone tour. "We didn't talk that much" on tour, Cabello told *Elvis Duran and the Morning Show*. According to her, Shawn spent the tour off on his own playing guitar and writing songs while the girls of Fifth Harmony were off having fun.

her and she's so talented. She's one of the sweetest girls I've ever met and super, super-smart."

With all the success Shawn has enjoyed in such a short time, the fame must be going to his head, right? Not so, says Hailee Steinfeld, who recorded an acoustic duet of "Stitches" with Shawn in 2015. "He's one of the most amazing guys I've ever met. He really is so sweet," the actress told Radio.com.

Not one to rest on his laurels, Shawn took the success of *Handwritten* and put his nose back to the grindstone, working on new music and training with vocal and instrument coaches to improve his abilities. All that while on a world tour *and* finishing up his high school studies. And in July 2016 he announced via Twitter that he had a new album already in the works and set to debut in just two short months. *Illuminate* was just around the corner... ★

Shawn shows off his stripped-down performance style: T-shirt, jeans, and guitar.

Everything Is "Illuminated"

Chapter Eight:
Everything Is "Illuminated"

OG fans of Shawn Mendes know he's got a great voice and a wide-ranging taste in music. Just look at his Vines, where he covers everyone from One Direction to Oasis to Katy Perry. But it's a well-known fact that the musicians he gravitates toward the most have a little less flash. They're singer-songwriters and guitar virtuosos like John Mayer and Ed Sheeran.

Shawn has often pointed out his admiration for Sheeran, whose musical talent inspired him early on. He covered several songs of Sheeran's on Vine and even onstage, including "Give Me Love," "Thinking Out Loud," and "The A Team." As a matter of fact, "The A Team" was the first song Shawn ever learned to play on the guitar. (Talk about ambitious!) He studied YouTube videos of Sheeran playing the song over and over until he had it figured out.

"I really look up to Ed Sheeran," Shawn told the online music channel VEVO. "He just has one guitar and he makes it sound like an entire band." And he strove to channel some of Sheeran's fullness into his sophomore album, *Illuminate*. "I'm playing more instruments. I'm trying vocally to show people what I've been learning," he told *Rolling Stone*.

And his "idol" and "rock god" is unequivocally John Mayer. Speaking about Mayer to Toronto's *Metro*, Shawn gushed, "His lyricism is just unreal, dude. The words me and the songwriters [of *Illuminate*] say are: 'What would John Mayer say?' *Continuum* is the album me and my best friends listen to in car rides or whenever we're hanging out. It's that well-rounded album that I know me and my friends can put on and no one's ever going to be angry about it. [It] always makes me so nostalgic and feel good when I'm home."

Being referential can often mean that you have big shoes to fill, but Shawn is up to the challenge. "I wanted to [make] an

---

AUGUST 8, 2016

THIS DAY IN SHAWN-STORY

Shawn turns 18 and the world swoons!

*J'adore Shawn!
Performing for fans
in Paris in 2016.*

Giving peace a chance while out and about in London.

album like [*Continuum*, which] kind of created friendships and bonds between people." By his own estimation, *Illuminate* is just that.

It's safe to say that Shawn's move toward more electric guitar-driven songs is a step closer to Mayer's musical style. Look no further than *Illuminate*'s "Ruin," which echoes the spare, bluesy riffs of Mayer's 2006 single "Gravity" from the multi-Grammy Award-winning album *Continuum*. (Not convinced? Shawn has said many times over that "Gravity" is his

THE BEST OF BOTH WORLDS

What do you get when you combine Ed Sheeran and Rupert Grint? Sheeran's "Lego House" video...and two of Shawn's faves in one!

"all-time favorite" song, so the homage makes perfect sense!)

He admits that the new album is ambitious, but it's also an honest reflection of who and where he is as an artist. "It's like my brain. It's like the inside look of my thoughts," he told *Rolling Stone*. So if fans

fanchat

"Watching him onstage and listening to him talk about his songs and what was going through his head while writing them, there was an intimacy and a feeling of love and pride that you can't feel by watching the concert two days later on YouTube... It was the best night of my life."

—Maggie Moyer, *Bucks County Courier Times*

Chapter Eight:
Everything Is "Illuminated"

are looking for a more personal glimpse into the artist and his life, this is it.

Mendes and his crew wanted to choose an apt place for quiet reflection and introspection. The album was written and recorded in the sleepy town of Woodstock in Upstate New York. Single-mindedly devoted to producing the album, Shawn tapped into his own experiences more than ever before. He explored his past romantic relationships (or relationship, single, he is quick to clarify) and the trials and tribulations that come with being a teenager. "I've had a crazy two years where the most inspiring things happened to me," he told MTV. "I feel like there's so

much to talk about, and I'm able to go into more detail with certain things in a more mature way."

It was exhausting work for Shawn, who dug deep not just emotionally but physically. "We were writing on the hills," he told *Entertainment Weekly*. "We'd wake up and go for a run, go to the gym, then write till nine o'clock at night. We'd take a break, eat dinner, then write till three a.m., producing and writing on repeat."

"It's so much more done by me" than his other releases to date, he told the Huffington Post. He not only had a hand in the writing and recording, but he followed the production process all the way through to the end. "For 90 percent of the songs I was standing beside the producer the entire song" while it was being mixed.

DREAM COLLABS

John Mayer and Ed Sheeran have collaborated on some of music's biggest stages. They performed Sheeran's "Thinking Out Loud" together at the 2015 Grammys (along with the Roots' Questlove). And while guest-hosting The Late Late Show, Mayer accompanied Sheeran on his searing "Don't." The pair actually have a bit of a bromance going. They even designed surprise tattoos for one another!

He's been slimed. He's won awards. He's won over critics and fans alike.

Shawn says he couldn't be any prouder of the result. "I'm way more confident with this album, it's not even funny. I mean, I just feel so good about it. If it sold no records, I'd still be so much more confident [as a musician]. I'm so passionate about the music I created that, if it sold 10 copies the first day, I'd still be happy," he said in an interview with the *Fader*. But when asked to pick a favorite song among the lot, Shawn balks. "I love all of them. They're like my children," he told *Rolling Stone*.

So far, the reception has been overwhelmingly positive. The album's first single, "Treat You Better," tackles some of the "edgy" material Shawn teased in preview interviews about the album. Along with its companion video, it addresses toxic relationships and domestic violence. But the dark subject matter hasn't scared off his fans. Rather, it's inspired a groundswell of support for bringing focus to difficult issues. To date, "Treat You Better" is his second-highest-charting single, trailing only "Stitches."

Chapter Eight:
Everything Is "Illuminated"

At the Macy's Thanksgiving Day Parade in New York, Shawn looks like he's on top of the world.

The full album was released September 23 with "Treat You Better" still racing up the charts. It's safe to say fans have been just as satisfied with the record as Shawn is.

Just 18 years old, and already leaps and bounds from where he began as a musician, Shawn is poised for a long and fruitful career. He works tirelessly day in and day out to get better as a guitarist, a songwriter, a performer, and a role model. It's a page he's taken from Taylor Swift, who arguably gave him his biggest break in the biz. "It seemed like she never stopped," he told the Huffington Post. "It was cool to see that somebody at that level of fame and success was still working so hard to be there. It showed me that there's no amount of success that allows you not to work hard."

There's no telling how far Shawn will go, but if his commitment to his craft is any indication, he has a very, very long road ahead of him. ★

UNDER THE INFLUENCE

	SHAWN	ED	JOHN
Age	18	25	38
Hails from	Canada	England	USA
Instruments played	Guitar, piano	Guitar, piano, bass guitar, cello, drums	Guitar
Learned to play guitar at age	13	Unknown, but his video "Photograph" shows him playing as a very young boy.	13
...after becoming inspired by	Watching YouTube videos of Ed Sheeran	Videos of Eric Clapton he saw at age 11	Watching Marty McFly play guitar in *Back to the Future*
Musical influences	These guys	Damien Rice, Eminem	Stevie Ray Vaughan, Jimi Hendrix, Eric Clapton
Released first album at age	15	20	23
Billboard 100 singles	6	8	16
Grammy Awards	None yet...	2	7
Unlikely collaborator	A$AP Rocky , Hailee Steinfeld	Everyone from Elton John to Hilary Duff to Pharrell Williams	Frank Ocean, Katy Perry

❝ Doing what you love for a living. ❞

—Shawn, when asked to define "success" by *Forbes* magazine